Amazing garden animals

What are baby hedgehogs called? Are really as sweet as they look? Find out

A long time ago, bats were called flittermice.

Honey bees die after they sting someone.

Baby hedgehogs are called hoglets.

Robins look cheery and sweet, but they
can be very aggressive.

Badgers are very clean animals. They
have toilet areas and rarely take
food into their homes.

You don't get boy and girl earthworms
and slugs – they are both in the same body.

You might find a slow worm in your garden.
It looks like a snake, but is in fact a lizard.

When at rest, dragonflies hold their wings out to the
side and damselflies press their wings together.

A fear of spiders is called arachnophobia.

hornet

Wildlife-spotters, turn the page!

Easy-to-spot garden wildlife

Look out for these animals in spring, summer
and autumn. It is too cold for most of them in winter.

peacock ◯

bumblebee ◯

blue tit ◯

rabbit ◯

aphid ◯

slug ◯

robin ◯

ladybird ◯

black ant ◯

LET'S LOOK FOR
GARDEN WILDLIFE

HOW TO USE THIS BOOK

Gardens are busy places, full of animals looking for food and bringing up their families. Many of them are hard to see and some only come out at night. Use this guide to...

...read all about the incredible creatures living in your garden and find out what is so amazing about them.

garden snail

Withdrawn from Stock
Dublin City Public Libraries

...ke outside with you to see what animals you can find and identify. Then tick off the ones you see.

...have fun playing with the wildlife stickers on the fold-out garden play scene at the back.

Looking for animals

Gardens are home to many different types of
animals. Here are some of the ones you may find.

Furry animals
Keep a look out for foxes, rabbits,
squirrels, badgers and mice.
They are often very shy.

Birds
Birds love gardens, especially
if you leave food out for them.
How many different
types can you see?

Creepy-crawlies
These are bugs with legs and you
can find lots of them in your garden.

Slugs and snails
You will probably
see more of these
on wet days.

Frogs, toads, snakes and lizards
These cold-blooded garden
animals can be quite tricky to
find. You'll be lucky to see any!

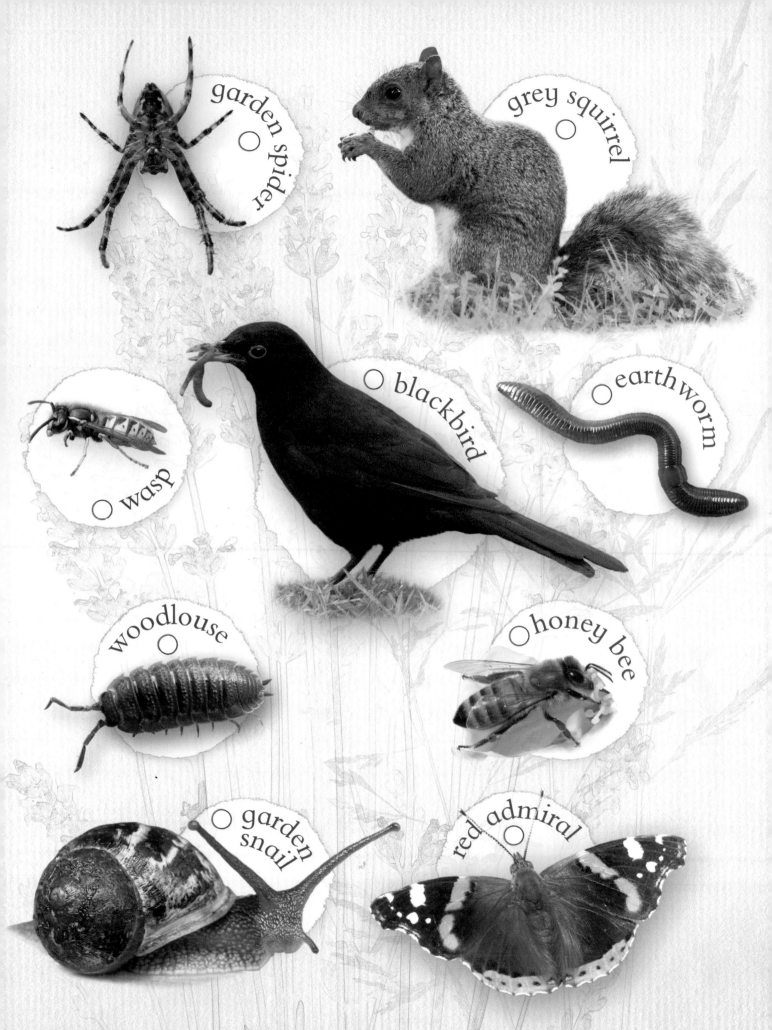

garden spider ○

grey squirrel ○

○ blackbird

○ earthworm

○ wasp

woodlouse ○

○ honey bee

○ garden snail

red admiral ○

Tick the animals off as you find them.

Hard-to-spot garden wildlife

○ common blue

beetle ○

common lizard ○

○ hornet

○ orange tip

○ magpie

common blue damselfly ○

banded snail ○

goldfinch ○

small tortoiseshell

caterpillar

shield bug

speckled wood

woodpigeon

burnet moth

hoverfly

grasshopper

frog

Who goes there?

When you are asleep, many garden animals appear. Ask an adult to take you out one evening to see what wildlife you can find.

Bats
Bats fly at night and sleep during the day.

Moths
The best place to find moths is near a light.

Cockchafer
These noisy insects are only around from May to July.

Stag beetles
Males use their large jaws for fighting.

Foxes
You have a good chance of seeing foxes in towns and the countryside.

Hedgehogs
These prickly animals may sleep through the winter.